ELLING

ELLING

based on the novel by Ingvar Ambjørnsen
in original stage adaptation by Axel Hellstenius
in collaboration with Petter Næss

in a new version by Simon Bent

OBERON BOOKS
LONDON

First published in this adaptation in 2007 by Oberon Books Ltd
521 Caledonian Road, London N7 9RH
Tel: 020 7607 3637 / Fax: 020 7607 3629
email: info@oberonbooks.com
www.oberonbooks.com

A catalogue record for this book is available from the British
Library.

Cover photograph by Robert Workman

ISBN: 1 84002 794 0 / 978-1-84002-794-5

Characters

for five actors

ELLING

KJELL BJARNE

ALFONS JORGENSEN

FRANK ÅSLI
also POET

REIDUN NORDSLETTEN
also GUNN, JOHANNE and POET

The main action of the play takes place in and around an apartment in Oslo. The present.

The basic set to begin with is two single beds centre stage, on the diagonal. One bed upstage left, with a wardrobe at some distance and further along the diagonal. The other bed downstage right. The foot of each bed facing downstage left corner. A low bedside cupboard by the side of both beds.

This adaptation of *Elling* was first performed on 27 April 2007 at the Bush Theatre, transferring to Trafalgar Studios in the West End on 6 July 2007, with the following company:

ELLING, John Simm
KJELL BJARNE, Adrian Bower
ALFONS JORGENSEN, Jonathan Cecil
FRANK ÅSLI, Keir Charles
REIDUN NORDSLETTEN, Ingrid Lacey

Director Paul Miller
Design Simon Daw
Lighting Mark Doubleday
Sound Jack C Arnold

KJELL: No.

ELLING: And all while I'm trying to eat a hard-boiled egg.

KJELL: Please, not any more.

ELLING: Sex.

KJELL: No.

ELLING: Mother won't have it in the house.

KJELL: I'm hard.

ELLING: Animal.

KJELL: Mommy's boy.

ELLING: Orangutan.

KJELL: I wish I was, then I'd be able to jump on any passing female orangutan and do what I want.

ELLING: It's clear to me that you need spiritual guidance.

KJELL: I need to get laid.

ELLING: You get tired of it. Unlike boiled eggs.

KJELL: I'd never get tired of fucking.

ELLING: Believe me. I'm a man of the world.

KJELL: You've seen the world.

ELLING: I know the world. I was third mate on the SS Norway. Came to a brothel in the Caribbean –

KJELL: With naked chicks.

ELLING: I impressed the negresses so much that they forgot to charge me.

KJELL: Holy shit! You must have a ton of stories.

ELLING: I do.

KJELL: Kjell Bjarne. I'm beginning to like you. (*Offers hand.*)

ELLING: Elling.

They shake

KJELL: You've got me that damn excited, I need to eat. Come on. And you can tell me more about the negress.

Act One

Two single beds

Small bedside cupboards (radio on one)

And a wardrobe

KJELL BJARNE wakes

Looks at empty bed opposite

Sheets ruffled

Looks around room

KJELL: Hello. Hello, is anyone there.

Gets up

Vest and pants

Looks under empty bed

Hello.

Looks at wardrobe

Goes toward it

Stands and looks at it

Hello.

Silence

As he reaches to open the wardrobe its door opens and out steps a man in pyjamas carrying a notebook and torch

ELLING: Good morning.

KJELL: Good morning. You like wardrobes.

ELLING goes to his bed

Puts notebook and torch under pillow

And starts dressing

ELLING: I don't want to miss breakfast.

KJELL: Bad night.

ELLING: No.

KJELL: That's not what it looked like.

ELLING: You were asleep.

KJELL: I don't sleep.

ELLING: That's not what it sounded like.

KJELL: I don't snore.

ELLING: You snore.

KJELL: What was that you put under your pillow.

ELLING: Nothing. My notebook. It's private.

KJELL: Nothing's private in here.

KJELL goes to exit

ELLING: Where are you going.

KJELL: Breakfast.

ELLING: You're not getting dressed.

KJELL: I am dressed.

ELLING: Elling.

Offers hand

KJELL doesn't take it

KJELL: Kjell Bjarne.

ELLING: I'm your new roommate.

KJELL: I know. The last one died.

ELLING: When I arrived you were asleep.

KJELL: I don't sleep. What are you here for.

ELLING: Nothing.

KJELL: Hell, you too. We must be the only two sane people in this nuthouse.

ELLING: The government generously supplies places – for people who are in a…hectic phase in their lives. After some coercion I accepted.

KJELL: I was jumped on by six policemen, tied up in a straitjacket, thrown in the back of a paddy wagon and beaten unconscious.

ELLING: I should have declined the offer.

KJELL: The biggest damn policemen you ever saw.

ELLING: Now total strangers want to talk to me about my life.

KJELL: I tell no lie. All twelve of them.

ELLING: Don't they have lives of their own to talk about.

KJELL: Fifteen police officers and me in the back of a paddy wagon, with no trousers on.

ELLING: They took off your trousers.

KJELL: No, I had to make a proposal and it didn't feel right doing it with them on. I've never liked trousers much.

ELLING: You made a proposal.

KJELL: Yes. Marriage. To a woman.

ELLING: And what did she say.

KJELL: She called the police.

ELLING: You had a lucky escape.

KJELL: I'm almost forty and I've never fucked.

ELLING: You have half your life ahead of you.

KJELL: I have half my life behind me.

ELLING: It's been glamourised.

KJELL: Glamourised.

ELLING: Without question.

KJELL: The only question I have is, when am I going to get it.

ELLING: It's about survival. A neccessity. Without it we die.

KJELL: I know.

ELLING: Sex.

KJELL: Don't.

ELLING: It's everywhere.

KJELL: Please.

ELLING: Even the news, breakfast televison presenters provocatively arousing the nation –

ELLING: I'll be down later.

KJELL: You won't forget.

ELLING: I won't forget.

KJELL: And don't go changing rooms.

ELLING: We are friends now Kjell Bjarne. We shook on it.

KJELL: I've never had that many friends.

ELLING: Me neither. None actually.

KJELL: Goddam. Last night I was alone and today – I have to
eat. Watch out for Gunn. Don't let her find that notebook
under your pillow.

ELLING: Who's Gunn.

Exit KJELL (ELLING now fully dressed)

Forgive them mother for they know not what they do.

Turns on radio: 'Zeiligheit' ('Happiness') by Schubert

Opens wardrobe

Takes out suitcase

Puts suitcase on bed

Opens it and puts pyjamas in it

Returns to wardrobe

Takes out coat and puts it on

Enter a nurse (ELLING's back to her)

Turns off radio

ELLING turns

Gunn.

GUNN: You have been with us two years now Elling. And
today you and Kjell Bjarne are leaving.

ELLING: That is correct. After two years of sharing a room
together the Norwegian government has decided to give us
an apartment of our own, in the centre of Oslo. From there
we shall attempt to return to reality.

GUNN: I found this.

Takes out a notebook

ELLING: Kjell Bjarne and I have a train to catch.

GUNN: There are plenty of trains.

ELLING: No. We have to catch this one. We have to meet Frank Åsli. He works for the government.

GUNN: Kjell Bjarne may well not want to catch a train with you after he has heard what I have to say. Sit.

ELLING sits

Whose notebook is this.

ELLING: I don't know.

GUNN: Does it look familiar.

ELLING: No.

GUNN: Look under your pillow why don't you.

ELLING: What for.

GUNN: Stop playing with me Elling.

ELLING: I am not playing. I never play, Gunn.

GUNN opens notebook

GUNN: (*Reads.*) 'Gunn is a sadistic mindless bully, with a brain the size of a pea, as qualified to work in such an establishment as is a brush with only one bristle useful to sweep a floor.'

ELLING: Really.

GUNN: Pages of abuse. I found it under your pillow.

Enter KJELL (fully dressed, coat on)

KJELL: Ah, Gunn you've come to say goodbye.

ELLING: No, Kjell Bjarne. Gunn has come to stop us.

GUNN: Sit down.

KJELL sits

Do you know whose notebook this is.

KJELL looks at ELLING

KJELL: Elling.

ELLING shakes his head

No. We've got a train to catch.

GUNN: (*Reads.*) 'I have always been a mommy's boy
I am an only child, as is mother
We enjoyed each other's company
No one ever came to visit
But when mother died, they came.
They want to talk
Talk about mother and me and our
intense two-ness through the years.
My roommate is an orangutan
Who cares only about women and food.
One of life's simpler apostles...
...
Kjell Bjarne likes my stories so much
I will make one up for him every day'

Stops reading

Elling has lied to you, Kjell Bjarne.

KJELL: Lied.

GUNN: Can you really trust in sharing an apartment with a man who considers you to be an orangutan.

KJELL: I know I'm an orangutan.

GUNN: And lies to you. If you fail in this rehabilitation programme you will not be given another chance and will spend the rest of your days institutionalised. Can you really put your faith in this man. How can you trust a man who lies so easily.

ELLING: They're not lies. They're stories.

GUNN: Well Kjell Bjarne.

KJELL: So you're not in the Bandidos.

ELLING: I'm not exactly a member.

KJELL: And that chick you fucked on a bike.

GUNN: Lies.

ELLING: You're just jealous, Gunn.

KJELL: The lady on the tropical island that rubbed you and herself in with…

ELLING: Coconut oil.

GUNN: Another lie. Well Kjell Bjarne.

Silence

KJELL: I don't give a damn.

ELLING: Do you mean that.

KJELL: Sure. As long as you tell them all again.

ELLING: My book, please Gunn.

GUNN: You'll be back. And soon. I can wait.

Exit GUNN with radio

KJELL: You think I'm simple.

ELLING opens book and gives it to KJELL

ELLING: There.

KJELL: (*Reads.*) 'My roommate is an orangutan
Who only cares about women and food
One of life's simpler apostles
But I feel safe in some strange way
Having him by my side.'

Gives book back to ELLING

Let's get some beers for the train.

KJELL picks up suitcase and exits

Beds parted

On opposite sides

ELLING's upstage left with wardrobe

Foot of the bed facing downstage

KJELL's downstage right

Foot of the bed facing opposite side stage left

Each with bedside cupboard

ELLING centre stage

Suitcase at feet

Sound of railway station

Trains tannoys people etc

As he stands alone and during the following speech the sounds intensify and get louder

ELLING: I am not alone... I am waiting... I am waiting for my friend Kjell Bjarne... Yes, thank you. I am fine... Where to? –

Kjell Bjarne and I are of course going to Oslo... One way?

Are there other ways... The quickest way to Oslo... Yes, I am sure. He will be back. I am not alone We are going to be met by Frank Åsli... You work for the government too.

Are you generally nice people... One hundred and thirty kroner each... The last time I took the train it cost twenty-five kroner each... Yes, that was twenty years ago... I am not alone, I am waiting, I am waiting for my friend...

Enter KJELL with suitcase

KJELL: Elling.

Noise stops

ELLING: Kjell Bjarne.

KJELL: Who are you talking to.

ELLING: No one.

KJELL: You were talking to yourself.

ELLING: You were gone too long.

KJELL: I said you could come.

ELLING: Public toilets aren't my forte.

KJELL: I met a man.

ELLING: I have no wish to know.

KJELL: We got talking.

ELLING: What did he say.

KJELL: He asked where we were going

ELLING: And you told him.

KJELL: Oslo.

ELLING: What if he follows us.

KJELL: He won't.

ELLING: How can you be sure.

KJELL: He said he was going to Russia.

ELLING: For what purpose.

KJELL: I can't.

ELLING: Tell me.

KJELL: Sex.

ELLING: Such an obvious lie. Why go to Russia with all the problems that entails when he can so easily go to Thailand.

KJELL: Please don't say that word.

ELLING: Sex is something we all have to come to terms with.

KJELL: That country. The best damn food and chicks in the world.

ELLING: Cabbage soup and women with too much make-up.

KJELL: Thailand.

ELLING: You met a man obviously up to no good in a public convenience and did not realise it. You are an innocent. The world is a dangerous place Kjell Bjarne.

KJELL: I don't trust myself.

ELLING: With every good reason. Trust no one.

Exit ELLING and KJELL

Music: Stone Roses, 'So Young'

Enter FRANK ÅSLI

Table centre stage

Three chairs upturned on it

And radio

FRANK sets chairs at table

Sits at table

FRANK takes out cigarettes and lighter

RADIO: That's it old rockers, no more smoking in public places, that's Oslo for you – we've got a law for everything – Imagine what it's going to be like in winter when there's snow in the street. Give up.

FRANK: Swivel on that.

FRANK tries to light cigarette

Repeatedly flicks lighter

RADIO: The World Health Organisation says that tobacco kills four point nine million people every year or one every six point five seconds.

FRANK: (*Shakes lighter.*) Bugger.

Repeats flicking

RADIO: Right-handed? Trying to quit. Having trouble. Here's a tip – start holding it in your left hand –

Turns off radio

FRANK: Fascists.

Puts cigarette behind ear.

Puts radio on bedside cupboard upstage left

Returns to table

Places two sets of keys on it

Doorbell

Come in.

Doorbell

I said come in.

Doorbell

It's open.

Enter KJELL BJARNE

KJELL: (*Shouts off.*) Elling.

FRANK: You got here alright.

KJELL: Elling.

Enter ELLING

FRANK: Hey, Elling and Kjell Bjarne. You boys have been on a trip.

ELLING: Are you…Frank Åsli.

KJELL: Do they have hot dogs here.

FRANK: How was your trip.

ELLING: I'm dying.

KJELL: What's your name again.

ELLING: Frank Åsli, Kjell Bjarne.

KJELL: And you are a social worker.

FRANK: That's right.

KJELL: Are you married, Frank Åsli.

FRANK: Yes.

KJELL: Is she nice, Frank Åsli.

FRANK: Nice enough. Call me Frank.

KJELL: What's her name, Frank.

ELLING: Kjell Bjarne.

KJELL: Does she have any girlfriends.

ELLING: Kjell Bjarne.

KJELL: Nice apartment you got here, Frank.

FRANK: It's not mine.

KJELL: Whose is it.

FRANK picks up keys off table and holds them up

FRANK: Make yourselves at home, boys.

KJELL: Holy shit. Elling.

KJELL and ELLING take their key

FRANK takes cigarette from behind ear

FRANK: Either of you got a light.

ELLING: Smoking is banned in all public places. On our way here we passed a small group of disgruntled smokers throwing rotten tomatoes at parliament.

FRANK: This isn't a public place.

ELLING: No. It's our new home.

FRANK: It's up to you to prove you can live alone. Shop, cook... Answer the phone. Prove that you can live normal lives. If you fail, there are plenty of people waiting for this apartment.

KJELL: There's no food here.

FRANK: No. You have to get it yourself. Out the door, down the street to the left. I'll be checking on you. Things should go according to plan. And you each get your own bedroom.

Points upstage left

That's your room, Elling.

Points downstage right

And you go down there, Kjell Bjarne. The kitchen's over there.

Points downstage left

And the bathroom there.

Points upstage right

Now go and put down that damn luggage.

KJELL: Yes, Frank.

KJELL goes to his bed taking his suitcase with him

ELLING: Yes, Frank.

ELLING goes to his bed

FRANK: Here's my phone number.

KJELL puts down his suitcase

KJELL: This is my room.

FRANK: I leave it on the table.

Puts card on table

KJELL: I have a room of my own.

FRANK: Yeah, great isn't it.

ELLING: Great, Frank Åsli.

KJELL and ELLING return to centre stage

ELLING still with his suitcase

FRANK: My number. But remember, I have ten others to care for.

ELLING: Jesus also had twelve people to take care of.

FRANK: Let's go out and get something to eat.

ELLING: You want us to go out, Frank Åsli.

FRANK: You need to eat.

KJELL: I need to eat.

ELLING: We've only just come in.

FRANK: The state's dollar.

ELLING: We've been out all day.

KJELL: Come on, Elling.

ELLING: We only just arrived.

KJELL: The state is buying us dinner.

ELLING: We just got here.

KJELL: We don't have anything to eat.

ELLING: Why go out.

FRANK: To celebrate your new home.

ELLING: Why not celebrate our new home in our new home.

FRANK: You want to stay in, Elling.

ELLING: Yes, Frank Åsli.

FRANK: Then, you go out and buy the food.

FRANK gives ELLING cash

And get me some matches.

Silence

KJELL: I'm hungry.

FRANK: We're waiting.

ELLING: I'll go then.

FRANK: Yes, go.

ELLING: I'm going.

FRANK: Goodbye.

ELLING turns and walks upstage

I'll order a pizza, he'll never make it.

Spotlight on ELLING

Stops turns facing downstage

ELLING: I have two enemies, dizziness and anxiety. Now I have a third, Frank Åsli. It's bright. Too bright.

Puts on sunglasses

Back straight – knees forward – head up – heel down, push forward, swing arm.

Steps forward

And again, the next foot –

Steps forward

And again –

Steps forward

And so on and so on –

Walks a few awkward steps

Stops

A little girl. I can't move. She's skipping. She's smiling.

It's a little girl. Swinging something in her hand. Coming towards me. No.

Flinches sideways

Uh. A doll. It was a doll. I can't move, I'll never get there – I'm going nowhere, I'm getting nowhere – the pavement goes on for ever – I can't – I must – I will –

ELLING collapses

KJELL: Elling.

FRANK and KJELL rush to ELLING

Help him up

ELLING: I'm fine. I'm fine, Frank. Just fine. This is social worker Frank Åsli everyone.

They sit him at table

FRANK and KJELL sit

Mother did all the shopping, I was in charge of ideology.

Doorbell

KJELL: What's that.

ELLING: The doorbell.

KJELL: Who is it, Frank Åsli.

FRANK: The pizza-man.

KJELL: He's a friend of yours.

FRANK: No. I ordered a pizza and they deliver it.

KJELL: Holy shit. Do they do that with hot dogs, Frank.

Doorbell

ELLING: Don't look at me.

FRANK: I don't live here.

ELLING: I've been out.

Doorbell

KJELL: I'll answer the door.

Exit KJELL

FRANK: Better to have failed trying, than to have failed and never tried at all.

ELLING: I'm not finished yet, Frank.

FRANK: That's the spirit.

ELLING: I appreciate your enthusiasm, Frank.

FRANK: People would pay good money to get their hands on this apartment.

ELLING: What are you saying, Frank.

FRANK: Nothing.

ELLING: You can't take this away from us, Frank.

FRANK: It's up to you.

Enter KJELL with pizza box

KJELL: Holy shit. I opened the door and he said 'Pizza', and I said 'Yes', and then we just stood there looking at each other and he said 'You ordered a pizza', and I said 'No', and then he said 'This is the second floor apartment', and I said 'Yes, I live here', and then he said, 'This is your pizza then', gave me the pizza, put on his crash helmet and left.

Pizza box on table

KJELL opens it

Goddam.

KJELL takes a piece and eats

FRANK takes a piece and eats

FRANK: Elling.

ELLING: No, thank you Frank.

KJELL: The best damn pizza I ever had.

FRANK: Take a piece, Elling. You have to eat something.

ELLING: No one can order me to eat, Frank.

FRANK: You didn't move here to sit and stare at the wall.

ELLING: I'm not staring at the wall, I'm watching you eat.

KJELL: Are you sure they don't do this for hot dogs, Frank.

ELLING: You see, Frank – you don't have to go out for food.

FRANK: Yes, you do. You do. I expect you to go out again.

ELLING: Going out is not my forte.

FRANK: I'd like to see what your forte is.

ELLING opens suitcase and stands photograph on table
What's that.

ELLING: Mother. I'm decorating our apartment.

FRANK: With a picture of your mom. Hardly.

ELLING: Do you have a picture of your mom, Kjell Bjarne.

KJELL: Decorate with my mom.

ELLING: Yes. Or have you converted to the degenerate cause of promiscuity, liberalism and the degradation of family values, along with your new-found, cigarette-smoking, unshaven, unkempt friend Frank Åsli. Who probably listens to jazz. Well do you, Frank. Do you listen to jazz.

FRANK: Elling, take a grip.

ELLING: A grip of what, Frank – the modern world has left very little to take a grip of. Mother and I are in agreement that the Norwegian Labour Party was an excellent judge of right and wrong.

KJELL: If my mom showed up here, I'd throw her and my stepdad out on their backsides.

ELLING: Your mother gave birth to you, fed you, washed your clothes.

KJELL: Not my mom. I only ever wanted to kill her.

FRANK: That's good, Kjell Bjarne.

ELLING: 'Good', 'good', you praise him for bad thoughts.

FRANK: Better to own them than to pretend they don't exist.

ELLING: 'Own', Frank, 'own' – Kjell Bjarne does not own these thoughts, he did not purchase them in a shop, he made them up.

KJELL: Have you never wanted to kill your mother.

24

FRANK: Good question, Kjell Bjarne.

ELLING: 'Good'. 'Good'. First, why would I want to kill mother. And second – second – does the government know that you endorse genocide, or is that their policy.

FRANK: How about your dad.

KJELL: Was he nice.

ELLING: Father died forty-eight hours before I was born, but mother has always maintained that she liked him and we attach no blame to his death.

FRANK: 'We'. 'We'.

ELLING: Yes 'we', mother and I. I know this may come as a shock to you Frank but I love my mother.

FRANK: So, did Oedipus.

ELLING: Oedipus is a made up story.

KJELL: Is he one of your stories, Elling.

ELLING: No.

KJELL: Did he get to sleep with any chicks.

ELLING: Yes his mother.

KJELL: That's not true, tell me it's not true Frank Åsli.

ELLING: It's a made up story.

FRANK: And your mother is dead.

Silence

ELLING: The blame for which does not rest entirely at her feet. Was it really so very necessary for God to take her from me. Let us consider it for a moment, in relation to His own family. A not too dissimilar situation. An only son, an absent father –

FRANK: Your mother was not a virgin.

ELLING: A minor detail of difference. But the core facts remain the same. And what happened to the son.

FRANK: He was crucified.

ELLING: My point exactly. He had a clear purpose and was allowed to achieve it. But more importantly, and a fact overlooked by scholars and theologians, the son dies before the mother.

KJELL: That's sad.

ELLING: Sad for the son, true. But the mother is left to mourn, happy in his achievements, free to live the rest of her life without the worry of how her child will continue after her death.

FRANK: You believe your mother was a virgin.

ELLING: No, I already said – she was simply not herself at the moment of conception.

KJELL: Don't.

ELLING: Sex.

KJELL: Don't say that. I'm hard.

ELLING: But for that momentary hedonistic lapse, but for which mother has always told me she would have become a nun. I always tell her it's never too late. But she wouldn't go.

FRANK: And now she's gone for good.

ELLING: She took her responsibility as a parent seriously. How very unlike the modern world.

FRANK: It's the responsibility of parents to allow their children to grow up.

ELLING: Which mother has done wonderfully. She educated me. She fed me. She clothed me. I am expected to repay that with unkindness, to leave her at the drop of a hat, for some floozy when she gives me a wink and flashes me the seams of her stockings in her shiny high heels.

KJELL: Please.

ELLING: The tart. Leave mother for another woman. Never.

FRANK: So, you like men.

ELLING: Don't be ridiculous. True, I have done my fair share of 'male bonding' as we were taught to say in the hospital. For which I am grateful, and I don't mind who hears me say it. An open and frank statement of fact, a tribute to the expertise and professionalism of government workers. Workers not members, there is a difference, Frank – you do not rule the country. Yes Kjell Bjarne and I are men, we like each other, we have shared a bedroom, at times we have even got into the same bed Frank. What is there to be ashamed of, unless you fear something. We have re-entered the community as cititizens. But I will never betray mother for another woman.

FRANK: You're a grown man.

ELLING: And I know right from wrong.

FRANK: Your mother's dead.

ELLING: For which you seem to think she is culpable of some act of negligence.

FRANK: You don't need her to continue living. If you did, when she died then you would have died also. But she did and you did not.

ELLING: I'm in a state of mourning.

KJELL: I'm just in a state.

ELLING: As such, it ill behoves me to go out until such time as I have completed the grieving process.

FRANK: Go out or get thrown out, the choice is yours. You're on your own from now on boys.

FRANK stands

Picks up a slice of pizza

Bon appétit.

Takes a mouthful

And, bonne chance. Au revoir.

KJELL: Where are you going, Frank.

FRANK: I've got work to do.

ELLING: People to meet, lives to ruin, he's a social worker, Kjell Bjarne.

FRANK: Apartments like these are in short supply.

Exit FRANK

KJELL: You don't like him.

ELLING: He doesn't like me.

Silence

Why go out when we've got all this space inside.

KJELL: It's big.

ELLING: And it can be bigger.

ELLING puts photograph of mother back in suitcase

ELLING closes pizza box

Holds it out to KJELL

There's a chute in the hall.

Exit KJELL BJARNE with pizza box

We don't need anyone's permission to do anything anymore Kjell Bjarne, least of all Frank Åsli. This apartment belongs to us not him. This apartment is ours not Frank Åsli's, we can do what we want.

Enter KJELL BJARNE

KJELL: Yeah, we'll bring some chicks back.

ELLING: All in good time.

KJELL: You don't want to.

ELLING: There's no rush.

KJELL: You're right, we should sleep first. The biggest damn rubbish chute I ever saw, it nearly took my arm off.

ELLING: How much more space do two grown men need.

KJELL: Frank Åsli said we should go out.

ELLING: Frank Åsli, is a danger to our future security and happiness Kjell Bjarne. We should get rid of him as soon as we can.

KJELL: How do we do that.

ELLING: I'll have to think.

ELLING picks up his suitcase

KJELL: Now where are you going.

ELLING: To sit in my room.

KJELL: Good idea. Then we get some chicks.

KJELL follows ELLING

ELLING: You have your own room to sit in.

KJELL: Yes.

ELLING goes to his bed
KJELL goes to his bed
Both at the same time
Put their suitcases by their beds
Look at the bed
Test the mattress with their hand
Take off their coats
Roll up their sleeves and pace the room
Sit on the edge of their beds
Lie down
Roll over
Roll over again
Sit up
Sit on the edge of their beds
Silence

Elling.

Both run from their beds towards centre stage
Stopping short at the sight of each other

ELLING: Yes, Kjell Bjarne.

KJELL: I can't sleep.

ELLING: You don't sleep.

KJELL: No.

Silence

ELLING: Yes.

Both turn back to their rooms

Kjell Bjarne.

Both stop and turn to each other

I have been thinking. And we are missing something. Something that all civilised homes require in the advent of visitors. A spare room. There is only one thing we can do –

KJELL: Holy shit, that's the best damn idea I ever heard.

ELLING: My bedroom. I'll give you a hand.

They go to KJELL's bed

And push.

KJELL: Frank won't be able to complain about this, I bet Frank and his wife have got a spare room.

They push KJELL's bed upstage

ELLING: Don't worry about Frank, I know how to deal with Frank.

Ignore him.

Bed in position next to ELLINGs

There. Hang up the coats Kjell Bjarne.

KJELL: Now I can sleep.

ELLING: Now we can sleep.

KJELL: Just like in the nuthouse.

ELLING: And we have a spare room.

KJELL: Yeah, somewhere for the chicks to sleep.

KJELL picks up radio

Turns it on

Pop music

ELLING turns it off

I want to listen, Elling.

ELLING: Sure, but not to that.

Turns on radio

There is only one station: NRK P1.

Music: 'Let's Call the Whole Thing Off', Billie Holiday

Act Two

Beds remain in position

ELLING's bed tidy

KJELL's a mess

Comics, clothes etc

ELLING at kitchen table writing in notebook

KJELL lying on floor centre stage

Reading a comic

Next to him a telephone on phone book

KJELL: Elling.

ELLING ignores him

I'm hungry.

ELLING ignores him

Goddam – do I have to come in that kitchen myself. You want that. You want me to come in the kitchen.

Silence

Right. I'm coming. I'm coming into the kitchen. Now. Right now. Do you hear. Do you hear me, Elling.

Silence

KJELL throws down comic

Sits up

Goddam. I warned you. Don't say I didn't warn you.

I'm coming.

Stands

Telephone rings

Enter ELLING from kitchen

ELLING: Don't answer it.

KJELL: We never do.

They watch the phone ring

What if it's important.

ELLING: They'll write.

KJELL: We never open any letters.

ELLING: Because they're not important.

KJELL: How do you know.

ELLING: Years of experience working for the National Security Services, monitoring terrorist transactions in the Middle East.

KJELL: You've never said.

ELLING: I can say no more, we were made to sign a confidentiality clause.

Phone stops ringing

See, wrong number.

KJELL: How do you know.

ELLING: I'm not at liberty to say.

KJELL: I'm hungry.

ELLING: There's no food.

KJELL: It's your turn to shop. You haven't been outside once in four weeks.

ELLING: I do other things.

KJELL: Like write in your notebook.

ELLING: Kjell Bjarne how many times do I have to tell you not to throw your comics on the floor.

KJELL: What do you write about.

ELLING: Nothing.

KJELL: You write about me.

ELLING: It's private.

KJELL: How can it be, if it's about me. Show me. I have a right to know.

ELLING: It doesn't concern you.

KJELL: Frank said we should go out.

ELLING: Frank Åsli is not our friend. Frank Åsli is an obstacle that we must dispose of as soon as we can.

KJELL: I'm hungry.

ELLING: Go to the shop.

KJELL: You go to the shop.

ELLING: I don't eat.

KJELL: You eat.

ELLING: No, I don't.

KJELL: Yes, you do.

ELLING: I don't. It's you, you that eats. I starve myself so that you can eat. I am your best friend.

KJELL: Goddam – why do you do that, why do you always make me feel so guilty.

ELLING: Because you know that I am right.

KJELL: We should go out. Go somewhere with chicks.

ELLING: Women like clean, shaved men, not fourteen-day-old sweat and –

KJELL: It hasn't been fourteen days. Ten, max.

ELLING: You have the odour of a Shanghai brothel.

KJELL: Right, that's the last time I go shopping.

Telephone rings

They watch it ring

After a while it stops

ELLING: Wrong number again.

Banging at door

FRANK: (*Off.*) Elling.

Banging

Kjell Bjarne. Are you in there.

Banging

Open this door.

34

ELLING: He'll go away.

Enter FRANK

FRANK: Why don't you answer the phone.

ELLING: It must be broken.

FRANK: I've been ringing for a week.

ELLING: It doesn't work. Why don't you believe me Frank, you never believe me Frank. Remember Frank, there's no such thing as a dirty book, only the mind that reads it.

FRANK picks up receiver

FRANK: There's nothing wrong with it.

ELLING: It must have been a fault on the line.

KJELL: Is that true about the dirty books.

ELLING: What do you say, Frank.

FRANK: You haven't been out.

ELLING: No, Frank – we've just got up.

FRANK: It's four o'clock in the afternoon.

ELLING: Yes, yes, yes it is Frank – and we've been out all night, haven't we Kjell Bjarne, till four o'clock this morning.

FRANK: Where.

KJELL: At a disco.

ELLING: Yes, a disco.

FRANK: Which one.

ELLING: Not just one Frank, many – many many discotheques, Kjell Bjarne and I danced the night away.

KJELL: And naked chicks.

FRANK: Shape up, boys. Stick to our agreements. Or ship out. I have to be able to reach you by phone. We'll just have to practise again.

KJELL: I have to organise my toolbox.

FRANK: No. When the phone rings, you pick up the receiver and say hello. Elling first. Let's pretend it's ringing. Ring. Ring. Answer the phone.

KJELL: Answer, Elling.

FRANK: Pick it up and say hello.

ELLING: It's not for me, it's for Kjell Bjarne.

FRANK: Come on, Elling.

ELLING picks up phone

ELLING: Hello.

FRANK: Hi, Elling. Frank here. How are you.

ELLING puts down phone

Ring. Ring. Ring. Ring. Ring. Ring. Ring. Ring. Ring. Ring. Pick up the phone. Pick it up.

ELLING picks up phone

ELLING: Hi, I'm thirsty. Likewise. Bye.

Puts phone down

FRANK: Great, Elling. One more time.

ELLING: Mother handled all our phone calls at home.

FRANK: Ring. Ring. Your mother is dead. Ring. Ring. This is your home. You have to answer.

ELLING picks up phone

KJELL: Say something, Elling.

FRANK: Talk, Elling.

ELLING: Hello, mother, it's me your son, I'm in hell.

ELLING slams down phone

It's not natural to talk into a piece of plastic to someone you can't even see.

FRANK: Or who's dead. You need to leave the apartment more.

ELLING: Why have an apartment if we have to leave it all the time.

FRANK: If you don't do as I say, you won't have an apartment.

FRANK goes to light a cigarette

ELLING: No smoking in here.

FRANK: And no more staying cooped up here. Time to tighten the reins. Final warning: I want to see progress or you're out.

Exit FRANK

ELLING: He sticks his nose in everything. Nothing is good enough. And he mocks my ideals.

KJELL: Why don't we try to go out, just the two of us.

ELLING: We have to get rid of him.

KJELL: I'm scared too, Elling. But we have money. And we only live once.

ELLING: I hope so, the concept of reincarnation has been troubling me.

KJELL: No women are going to come here when they don't know we live here.

ELLING: We don't have to go out to meet women, Kjell Bjarne. Frank deserves credit for one thing at least, for teaching us how to use the telephone.

ELLING opens phone book

KJELL: What are you doing

ELLING: Trust me.

KJELL: I do.

ELLING picks up phone and dials

Tomorrow we go out. We have to. Or lose everything. Each other.

ELLING: (*Phone.*) Hello. Yes.

KJELL: You'll be alright. I'll see you're alright.

ELLING: (*Phone.*) Yes.

KJELL: We'll go to the café around the corner.

ELLING: (*Phone.*) Yes.

KJELL: The other day they had pork and gravy.

ELLING: (*Phone.*) Yes.

KJELL: If things get bad, we can just walk home again.

ELLING: Or run. (*Phone.*) Yes.

KJELL: It's that simple.

ELLING: Here – it's for you.

Hands phone to KJELL

Exit ELLING

KJELL listens down phone

KJELL: Holy shit.

VOICE-OVER: I just love sex. I'm sitting here playing with myself. Touch my tits…

KJELL: I'm hard Elling, I'm hard.

Exit KJELL with telephone

Music: 'Je t'aime', Serge Gainsbourg

VOICE-OVER: Touch me – touch it – I'm wet – you're hot – it's big – you're big – give it me, please, I'm begging – I want it, I need it – Oh – Oh – Ohhh…you're so hot, baby

During which…

Table cleared and moved centre stage

Waitress (JOHANNE) covers it with gingham tablecloth and sets it for two

A chair is set downstage front right with its back to the audience

Ring of shop bell as KJELL enters in coat and hat upstage back centre

Enter JOHANNE downstage front left

As soon as they see each other lights dim

Both stop

JOHANNE bathed in light

KJELL: (*Shouts off.*) Elling.

Back to normal

Music stops

A middle-aged man (ALFONS) now sitting on chair downstage front right

His back to us

Reading a paper

Enter ELLING in coat upstage back centre

ELLING: I'm dying.

KJELL: You're not dying.

ELLING: I hope they have lots of pork and gravy.

KJELL: I can't wait. Come on.

JOHANNE by table

JOHANNE: Table for two.

KJELL: Yes, please.

She pulls out a chair

(*Aside.*) Best damn woman I ever saw.

ELLING: This had better be good.

KJELL takes off his hat

KJELL: Take off your hat.

ELLING: What if we have to leave in a hurry.

KJELL takes off ELLING's hat and gives it him

KJELL: We're stopping.

KJELL and ELLING sit

JOHANNE gives them menus

JOHANNE: Here you go.

KJELL: Thank you.

KJELL looks at menu

Shit. They don't have pork and gravy.

JOHANNE: Anything to drink.

ELLING: We're here for the pork and gravy.

JOHANNE: Today's special is stew.

ELLING: You said they had pork and gravy.

JOHANNE: We had pork and gravy yesterday.

KJELL: What about today.

JOHANNE: Stew.

ELLING: When will there be pork and gravy.

JOHANNE: Next week.

KJELL: (*Slams fist on table.*) Shit. No pork and gravy.

JOHANNE: Let me check with the chef.

Exit JOHANNE

KJELL: Don't give up too easy, Elling.

ELLING: I had my mind set on pork and gravy. To come all this way, for stew. Kjell Bjarne.

KJELL: What a woman.

ELLING: I am in need of relief.

Enter JOHANNE

JOHANNE: We have two helpings left.

KJELL: Yes, please.

JOHANNE: Anything else.

KJELL: What's your name.

JOHANNE: Johanne.

KJELL: Johanne.

ELLING: Thank you, Johanne.

KJELL: Yes, thank you.

JOHANNE: My pleasure. Let me get you some water.

KJELL: Yes, please.

Exit JOHANNE

What a woman.

ELLING: We have to leave, Kjell Bjarne.

KJELL: Why.

ELLING: I need the gentlemen's.

KJELL: It's over there.

ELLING: I can't. Public conveniences aren't my forte.

KJELL: Want me to come with you.

ELLING: No.

Enter JOHANNE with jug of water

KJELL: Look at that

Music: 'Je t'aime', Serge Gainsbourg

ELLING gets up from table and crosses quickly downstage front right

Stands just upstage of man reading paper (ALFONS)

Back to him and undoes fly

Meanwhile KJELL transfixed by JOHANNE as she comes to table. She reaches table puts jug on table. Music stops

JOHANNE: Your water.

KJELL: Thank you.

ALFONS folds paper

Slips it under arm gets up stands a distance and on the same line stage left of ELLING

Undoes his fly

ALFONS: How different people are. Some people ski solo to the North Pole – while some have to summon all their courage to cross a restaurant floor. That must be what is meant by breaking boundaries. The modern world.

Turns head to ELLING

Do you like poetry.

41

Silence

Nothing happening.

JOHANNE: Shall I pour.

ALFONS: Having problems.

KJELL: Whatever you think.

ALFONS raises right hand and clicks fingers

At which point JOHANNE picks up large tall glass off table and fills slowly from jug raising it as high as she can while pouring

While she pours ELLING looks down

Turns head to ALFONS and smiles

JOHANNE finishes pouring and sets glass back down on table in front of KJELL

JOHANNE: I'll get you your food.

KJELL: Thank you.

ELLING: (*To ALFONS.*) Thank you.

ALFONS zips himself up

ALFONS: That's all for today.

Exit ALFONS upstage centre back

Walks past KJELL as he goes

ELLING zips himself up

Crosses quickly back to KJELL

And sits at table

ELLING: There was a man, a man in the toilet – that man, the man just going out – I was having problems, as I usually do – to go in a public place – when he started talking, then clicked his fingers and I went, like that, no problem.

KJELL: What man.

ELLING: The man that just passed our table.

KJELL: There was no man.

ELLING: I saw a man.

KJELL: You made him up.

ELLING: No, I didn't.

KJELL: Another of your stories. That or you're losing your marbles.

ELLING: Yes, yes, another of my stories.

Enter JOHANNE

JOHANNE: Your food is on its way.

KJELL: Pork and gravy.

JOHANNE: It won't be long now.

KJELL: Best damn restaurant I've ever been in.

ELLING: It won't be as good as mother's.

KJELL: I can't wait.

JOHANNE: I'll fill it up for you.

Exit JOHANNE with water jug

KJELL: What a woman. Bet Frank would love to see us now.

ELLING: He wouldn't be satisfied – until we joined a table full of people from foreign cultures. We should almost call Frank and tell him we are here.

KJELL: Do it.

ELLING: I said almost.

KJELL: It's nearly Christmas, Elling.

ELLING: I know Kjell Bjarne.

KJELL: I can't wait. What have you got me.

ELLING: That would be telling.

KJELL: I'm making you something. I'm making you –

ELLING: No, don't tell me. Wait.

KJELL: I can't.

ELLING: You have to.

KJELL looks at watch

KJELL: Twenty-seven days, four hours, six minutes and fifteen seconds to go.

ELLING: Where's our dinner.

KJELL: Twenty-seven days, four hours, six minutes and two seconds.

ELLING: What's happened to dinner.

KJELL: Our first Christmas alone together. I can't wait.

ELLING: When we get home we'll make a phone call.

KJELL: To Frank.

ELLING: Before Frank.

KJELL and ELLING raise glasses

They clink

Music –

The following as voice-over tape

(During which next scene set, and downstage right chair is struck)

FRANK: Hello. Åsli.

ELLING: Frank. Hi, it's me.

FRANK: Elling.

ELLING: Yes. Kjell Bjarne and I have just grabbed some food at our local haunt. They have pork and gravy on Fridays. Kjell Bjarne took some persuading.

FRANK: Well done, Elling.

ELLING: But I got him round in the end.

FRANK: Well done.

ELLING: Yes, isn't it, Frank...

FRANK: Yes it is, Elling. You're doing well.

Music: 'Silent Night'

ELLING at table now downstage left

Chair behind it facing out front

Writing in his notebook

Radio by his side

Mid-centre downstage right a Christmas tree

A large parcel underneath it

Two chairs and at some distance face it

One centre stage right, one downstage left

KJELL BJARNE sitting on stage right chair

Telephone next to it

Silence

KJELL gets up

Combs his hair

Paces the room

Combs his hair

Sits

KJELL: I like the tree.

Silence

I prefer that it's plastic.

Silence

It feels more like Christmas. Hell, Elling what are you doing in the kitchen at a time like this.

KJELL gets up, combs his hair

Paces the room, combs hair

Sits

Stands

I can't wait any longer, Elling.

ELLING: It's only five o'clock.

KJELL: I didn't sleep, I couldn't sleep.

ELLING: You don't sleep.

KJELL: No, I don't. Last night I didn't, and that's for sure. I've been waiting all day.

ELLING: Finish your cake first, at least.

KJELL: It's finished.

ELLING: Comb your hair.

KJELL: I comb it any damn more and there'll be nothing left to comb.

KJELL picks up parcel and crosses to upstage right of ELLING

Here you go, Elling.

ELLING: For me.

Takes present and places it on table

KJELL: If you don't like it, I'll go kill myself.

ELLING unwraps parcel

A large well-made matchstick house

ELLING: Kjell Bjarne.

KJELL: Is it alright.

ELLING: Is it alright.

KJELL: I made it myself.

ELLING: It's beautiful.

KJELL: Out of matchsticks. I made it in my spare time. It's our house. That's our flat. And look look, Elling. There's you and me.

You're the yellow one. You like it.

ELLING: Do I like it, Kjell Bjarne. It's the best damn present I ever had.

ELLING takes a small parcel out of table drawer

Here is your present, Kjell Bjarne.

KJELL: For me.

ELLING: Yes, I didn't make it.

KJELL: A present.

ELLING: Merry Christmas.

KJELL: For me.

Takes present

Goddam.

ELLING: Try not to curse on Christmas.

KJELL unwraps it

KJELL: Holy shit! A pen, it's a pen.

ELLING: Yes, it's a pen.

KJELL: I can't believe it, I don't believe it, holy – holy – damn, damn – how did you know – see...

Tips pen upside down

And all her clothes come off.

ELLING: Would that it were so easy in real life.

KJELL: Holy shit, how did you know I wanted the blonde.

ELLING: I have gotten to know you, Kjell Bjarne.

KJELL: This is the best.

ELLING: Likewise.

KJELL: Can we make a phone call.

ELLING: Not on Christmas Eve, that would be blasphemy. Play with your pen.

A sudden threatening noise

Banging and clattering

ELLING turns off radio

Silence

KJELL: What was that.

ELLING: Ssssh.

KJELL: It came from outside.

ELLING: (*Whispers.*) Don't breathe.

KJELL: Something's out there.

ELLING: Don't move.

KJELL: They're at our door.

ELLING: They'll go away.

KJELL: What if they don't.

ELLING: Turn out the lights.

KJELL: This is our home.

ELLING: No, Kjell Bjarne –

KJELL: I'll give them what for.

ELLING: Don't leave me.

KJELL: I'm not.

> *Picks up Christmas tree and holds it like a club*
> Protection.

ELLING: No, Kjell Bjarne, no – don't.

> *Exit KJELL*
> *Silence*
> Kjell Bjarne.
> *Silence*
> Kjell Bjarne.
> *Enter KJELL*
> Well.

KJELL: It's a woman.

ELLING: What's she doing.

KJELL: Nothing. She's unconscious. Flat on her back outside our door. She must have fallen down the stairs. What shall we do.

ELLING: She's still breathing.

KJELL: Yes.

ELLING: Leave her.

KJELL: We can't. She's pregnant.

ELLING: Someone else will find her.

KJELL: I'll bring her in.

ELLING: No. We've nowhere to put her.

KJELL: The spare room.

ELLING: There's no bed.

KJELL: We'll soon put that right.

KJELL goes to his bed and starts to push it downstage right

Give me a hand. Help me Elling.

They push bed downstage front right

ELLING: What if the putative father turns up, he'll think we've abducted her.

Bed in position

KJELL: Put a chair by the bed. Do it, Elling.

ELLING: Yes, Kjell Bjarne.

Exit KJELL

ELLING places chair by bed

Enter KJELL carrying pregnant woman

Kjell Bjarne, put that woman down immediately before you do any damage.

KJELL: Relax, I've done this a hundred times with my mom.

Lies her down on bed

ELLING: Who is it.

KJELL: How would I know.

ELLING: Is she sick.

KJELL: She will be. Now she's just drunk.

ELLING: What's your name.

KJELL: She can't hear you, she's unconcscious.

ELLING: Alright.

KJELL mops her brow with a handkerchief

49

KJELL: It's clean.

ELLING: I know, I cleaned it.

KJELL: Look in her purse.

ELLING: I'm no thief.

KJELL: Look in her purse. Find out what her name is.

ELLING opens purse

Empty it.

ELLING goes through purse

ELLING: Reidun Nordsletten. She lives here. The apartment above. December twenty-fourth, nineteen…

KJELL: The same birthday as Jesus. Holy shit, today. And she's pregnant.

ELLING: She couldn't just be a little fat.

KJELL: Sure, there's some fat here. But inside the fat there's an astronaut floating around.

ELLING: I hope she hasn't hurt the baby.

KJELL: I'll sit with her till she wakes.

ELLING: We should just leave her.

KJELL: What if she's sick.

ELLING: We'll look in on her from time to time.

KJELL: I'll stay till she's better.

ELLING: You can't. You look like a rapist. You'll terrify her.

KJELL: Do you think she's an angel.

ELLING: You are acting foolishly, Kjell Bjarne. I'll tell Frank.

KJELL: Close the door behind you.

ELLING: I know how to use the telephone.

KJELL: Shut the door.

ELLING: What am I supposed to do.

KJELL: Go to bed.

ELLING leaves KJELL sitting by bed

KJELL closes his eyes and falls asleep

ELLING sits on chair centre stage

Rocking on his hands

ELLING: He won't listen – he doesn't listen – he never listens...
Three has always been an awkward number... Kjell Bjarne
is out of control... Kjell Bjarne has given up his heart...
Kjell Bjarne is in love... Frank Åsli must be informed at
once...

Puts phone on chair and dials

No...no...

Replaces receiver

The best damn present I ever had.

ELLING goes upstage

To single empty bed and wardrobe

Puts on pyjamas

Takes notebook and torch from under pillow

Opens wardrobe

Gets in

Closes door behind him

Silence

Radio suddenly comes on

Music: 'Jolene', Dolly Parton

KJELL wakes up

Turns off radio

KJELL: Elling. Elling.

REIDUN wakes

KJELL looks in their bedroom

Elling.

Stands before wardrobe

REIDUN gets up and walks into front room

51

Elling.

As he reaches to open wardrobe REIDUN calls

REIDUN: Hello.

KJELL BJARNE runs back into front room

Sees REIDUN

Silence

KJELL: Kjell Bjarne.

REIDUN: Where am I.

KJELL: You live here. The apartment above. We found you in
  the hall.

REIDUN: My head hurts.

KJELL: You fell.

REIDUN: I was drinking.

KJELL: It's your birthday.

REIDUN: Yeah.

KJELL: I brought you in.

Silence

Are you an angel.

REIDUN: No. You're the angel.

KJELL: Holy shit.

REIDUN: My head hurts.

KJELL: I'll help you up the stairs.

REIDUN: Who were you calling for just now.

KJELL: No one. A friend.

Silence

It's Christmas.

REIDUN: I know.

Silence

KJELL: I got a pen. See…

Tips pen

And all her clothes come off.

She laughs

Oh, I'm sorry.

REIDUN: You're funny.

KJELL: They say I was born like it.

REIDUN: Who.

KJELL: Everyone. As long as I can remember. 'There's nothing wrong with Kjell Bjarne, he's just a bit funny.'

REIDUN: I like it.

KJELL: Goddam.

REIDUN: Reidun Nordsletten.

KJELL: I know. What did you get for Christmas, Reidun.

REIDUN: I don't know yet. Maybe the best present I ever had.

KJELL: Holy shit. Everyone's getting what they want this Christmas. Elling, me, and now you.

REIDUN: Who's Elling.

KJELL: Just a friend.

REIDUN: You like coffee. I'll make you some coffee.

KJELL: I bet you make the best damn coffee.

REIDUN: And chocolate-chip cookies.

KJELL: Holy shit.

Exit REIDUN followed by KJELL

Wardrobe door opens

ELLING steps out

Puts on shoes

Coat on over pyjamas

Notebook and pen in pocket

Goes to kitchen table

Looks at matchstick house

ELLING: The best damn present I ever had.

Picks it up and drops it on floor

It smashes

Puts on sunglasses

And if I do not return Kjell Bjarne, if something bad happens to me Kjell Bjarne and I am found dead in the gutter it will be your fault Kjell Bjarne and you will feel bad and you will be guilty and you will be sorry and it will be too late. I will be gone. And then you will know.

Goes to exit

Stops and turns

Looks around room

Orangutan.

Exits

Interval

Act Three

Early morning

Enter ELLING

Coat sunglasses half-eaten hot dog

Goes to kitchen table

Takes off coat and glasses (still in pyjamas)

Puts hot dog on table

Lays notebook on table and pen

Goes to bed downstage right

And pushes it back upstage

ELLING: (*As he pushes.*) First I was…and then I was…it took all the strength I had… I spent oh so many nights… I will survive… I will survive… I will survive…

Bed in centre of stage

Enter KJELL

So, you've come back. Tail between your legs. And now you want me to forgive you.

KJELL: We've been invited to dinner.

ELLING: We.

KJELL starts banging his head with his fists

KJELL: Dinner – dinner –

ELLING: Stop doing that Kjell Bjarne.

KJELL: Dinner.

ELLING: Stop it, before you knock yourself out.

KJELL stops

She invited us both.

KJELL: Yes, she said I could bring a friend.

ELLING: Oh. I won't be able to come. I have a previous appointment.

KJELL: When.

ELLING: At the exact time of dinner.

KJELL: You don't know when dinner is.

ELLING: Some things are best kept private.

KJELL: You don't go out.

ELLING: You spent the night with a pregnant woman.

KJELL: We sat on her sofa and she talked. She opened her mouth and didn't stop. I didn't know it was possible for anyone to talk so much. We had coffee, we had chocolate-chip cookies, and cold hen.

ELLING: Chicken.

KJELL: Hen.

ELLING: And where did you sleep.

KJELL: I haven't.

ELLING: Animal.

KJELL: She only just stopped talking.

ELLING: While you sat up with a pregnant woman on her sofa all night, talking – I took my life in my hands and went out. I went out and found my vocation.

KJELL: I like her.

ELLING: What about her husband.

KJELL: She hasn't got one.

ELLING: A loose woman.

KJELL: She likes me.

ELLING: Any decent woman would have woke up and called the police. Terrified to wake up next to an orangutan.

KJELL: She said I was an angel.

ELLING: Not all angels are white.

KJELL: I'm hungry.

Crosses to kitchen table

ELLING follows

ELLING: Satan is also an angel, a fallen angel, the Prince of Darkness. Doesn't she read the papers. This town is full of muggers and rapists.

KJELL picks up piece of broken matchstick house

It broke.

KJELL: I'll fix it.

ELLING: Can you really mend so easily that which is broken.

KJELL: It's time for you to go to bed, Elling. I sure am. I have to fix her leaky plumbing later.

ELLING: She wakes up in a total stranger's bed and immediately asks him to fix her leaky plumbing. Did she give you a key, too, so you can come and go as you please. Kjell Bjarne, you are in love. I have to report this to Frank. You are out of control.

KJELL: Dammit, Elling. I'm going to bed.

KJELL goes to head of bed centre stage

ELLING follows at foot of bed preventing KJELL from pushing it downstage

Out of my way.

ELLING: No.

KJELL: I'm moving my bed into the spare room.

Over the next few lines they push bed back and forth

ELLING: I've decided we no longer need a spare room.

KJELL: It's my bedroom.

ELLING: I need a library.

KJELL: I want a workshop.

ELLING: Library.

KJELL: Workshop.

ELLING: I've always wanted a library.

KJELL: We need a workshop.

ELLING: I need a library. Orangutan.

KJELL chases ELLING around and over the bed

No – no – Kjell Bjarne – don't – Listen, listen to me – I have something important to say – please listen…

ELLING runs into the kitchen

Chased round table by KJELL

Grabs notebook off table

Runs back into front room

Jumps on bed

Listen.

KJELL: Truce.

ELLING: Truce. I have discovered my true vocation. It was in the night that the words struck me. It was as if they were written on the inside of my eyelids.

Reads notebook

'At first we crawl then stumble,
Along this rocky shore.
Footprints in the sand
Heading for the sun.
Last night I found an angel,
Fallen at my door
Her tousled hair, like wings –
Beating at the vinyl.
We were sent a fallen angel – with child –
Drunk upon the floor.
We do the best we can,
What more can be done?
All pilgrims crawl then stumble,
Along this rocky shore.
Footprints in the sand
Heading for the sun –
But when night comes
We're down again
Our time – is done,

> At the end – as in the beginning
> We have only just begun'

KJELL: Holy cow, Elling…you have committed poetry.

ELLING: My entire life I have walked the earth not knowing I am a poet. No wonder there have been certain misunderstandings – when my poetry, my own language, has laid undiscovered within me.

KJELL: Do you want that hot dog.

ELLING: A library.

KJELL: Goddam, Elling – why do you always win.

ELLING: Because I am right.

They move bed back upstage next to ELLING's
There.

KJELL: I'm hungry.

KJELL crosses to table

Sits and eats hot dog

ELLING: And I have made a friend. Purely by accident, stumbling alone in the dark I came across a modern poetry reading.

KJELL: A poetry reading.

ELLING: I entered. I was lost but my old enemies dizziness and anxiety were strangely absent.

Lights cross fade to spotlight on FEMALE POET upstage at microphone

FEMALE POET: I wrote these poems while sick with malaria in Cambodia.
'Cobweb
I lie and stare at the cobweb
Every time something gets caught
You tear it asunder again'

Applause

My next poem is 'Spider', it's about Fascism in all its forms.

'Oozing through a clogged mind
Clotted thought
Cloudy dreams
Treacle thick sweat drips
A tingling climbs the spine
A spider crawling up my neck
And deep inside my brain
Today the doctor came
Cold clinical click of the heels
He smiles
And I am gone'

Applause

Lights cross fade back

Man from restaurant (ALFONS)

Sitting on downstage right chair

Politely applauding

Smoking a cigar

Turns to ELLING

ALFONS: Strange, huh – the worse it is, the more they clap.

ELLING: And there he was, sitting at the bar.

KJELL: The man from the restaurant.

ELLING: Yes. Imagine my surprise, the coincidence. Cool as a cucumber, smoking a cigar.

KJELL: But there was no man. You made him up.

ELLING: No, Kjell, no I did not. He bought me a drink.

KJELL: You don't drink.

ALFONS: On me.

ELLING: Thank you. Elling.

KJELL: You shouldn't drink.

Lights cross fade to spotlight and microphone

MALE POET runs into spotlight

Grabs mic

MALE POET: Is anybody out there. Can you hear me Oslo. Yeah. Let's do it.

'I was never allowed to touch her breasts
But from down there
I could see it all on wash days
The prodigal son
I could have milked her
Sucked the rich sticky dew
Round firm nutrition
I didn't stand a chance
He ground her with his axle
Grinding on her rim
Each night he put it in
And buried her in bed
The chassis groaned
Cracked and fell to snap
Brittle wood bled its dry sap
And always lurking in my mind
The faint taste of a sealed taboo
"Mom, do you suck cock"'

Let's hear it for Oslo. Yeah. Let go. Elvis is in the building.

ELLING: (*Shouts.*) Stop.

Lights back to normal (Microphone and MALE POET gone)

(*To KJELL.*) I was sick.

ALFONS: (*To ELLING.*) You too. Come on, let's get out of here.

KJELL: You're making this up, it's another of your stories.

ELLING: No, no, it's not.

ALFONS: So that made you sick, too. The worse it is, the more they clap. Cigar.

ELLING: No, no thanks. I don't.

ALFONS gives ELLING cigar

ALFONS: Take it. Give it to a friend.

ELLING puts it in pyjama top pocket

Want to go somewhere for a drink. Throw dirt on contemporary poetry.

ELLING: (*To KJELL.*) Why didn't I just say yes.

ALFONS walks upstage left and stops at the wings

KJELL: You're making this up.

ELLING: Don't be absurd Kjell Bjarne, why would I make such a thing up. It is now clear to me that I must become a mysterious underground poet – E: mommy's boy, maybe, but a new, dangerous version. All I need to do is find the right forum for my poetry.

ALFONS turns round

ALFONS: There you are again.

ELLING: (*To KJELL.*) Another chance encounter.

ALFONS turns to wing

ALFONS: Two hot dogs with mustard, please.

ELLING: (*To KJELL.*) I could feel the hand of destiny.

ALFONS turns with two hot dogs

ALFONS: Let's walk.

I've never met a man before whose physical reaction to modern poetry so aptly expresses my own literary views on the subject – vomit.

ELLING: I happen to like lyrical poetry.

ALFONS: Me too. Deeply unfashionable.

ELLING: I am. Also, I'm allergic to alcohol. It can make me do things I'll regret. I drank some liquor once, with some other boys.

Mother came home, and I did something I still regret.

I tore off her wedding ring and tried to sell her body to these 'friends'.

ALFONS: Lousy friends. Want one.

ELLING: Yes.

ALFONS: A hot dog.

ALFONS gives ELLING hot dog

ELLING: Thank you.

ALFONS: Do you go to poetry readings often.

ELLING: I've lived a sedate life until now. I rarely go anywhere.

ALFONS: Me neither. You shall have to change all that.

ELLING: And I have never been able to speak to strangers
before.

ALFONS: You're no stranger.

ELLING: (*To KJELL.*) And he was right. It was like I'd known
him all my life. Like he could see inside me. Almost as
if he had always been there. Just waiting for the right
moment to introduce himself. Mostly we just talked shop.

ALFONS: Madness is poetry's most important source.

*ELLING puts half-eaten hot dog down on table and picks up
notebook*

ELLING: (*To KJELL.*) I almost showed him my poem then
and there. But as an underground poet I had to remain
anonymous.

ALFONS: The urge to create goes hand in hand with the urge to
destroy. This is where we part. Thank you for wasting your
time on an old man.

ELLING: I never had a father.

ALFONS: Some people have all the luck.

ELLING: They call me Elling.

ALFONS: This was fun. Some people just pretend, but you
really are crazy.

ELLING: (*To KJELL.*) I was under the distinct impression that
this man needed cheering up. So I gave him my phone
number.

Opens notebook

(*To ALFONS.*) I'm going to give you my phone number.

Writes number

ALFONS: You keep a diary.

ELLING: Of sorts.

Tears page out

Gives it to ALFONS

There. Call me.

ALFONS: Inside the mind of a madman.

ELLING: Who is.

ALFONS: No one. Just a thought.

ELLING: Call me.

ALFONS: Don't worry, you'll be seeing me again. That's for sure.

Exit ALFONS

ELLING: I have made a friend. On my own. Without the aid of the Norwegian government.

KJELL picks up half-eaten hot dog

KJELL: It's a story.

Bites into hot dog

ELLING: You're jealous.

KJELL: You made him up.

ELLING: That hot dog's not made up.

KJELL: So what. And it's cold.

ELLING: You think I'm losing my mind.

KJELL: You've got your shoes on.

ELLING: Since when has wearing shoes been a sign of ill health.

KJELL: You've got your pyjamas on.

ELLING: I like my pyjamas. You don't like trousers.

KJELL: You went out in your pyjamas.

ELLING: There wasn't time to change.

KJELL: What's his name.

ELLING: I don't know.

KJELL: Where does he live.

ELLING: I don't know.

KJELL: When are you going to see him again.

ELLING: I don't know. I gave him my number.

KJELL: Did he give you his.

ELLING: You think I'm losing my mind

KJELL: You got drunk, that's all. You had a drink, bought a cigar, got two hot dogs on the way home and dreamed him up.

ELLING: You think I'm losing my mind.

KJELL: No. No. Not at all.

ELLING: It's starting again – no, no, there's nothing wrong with me, I didn't imagine it, I couldn't – I'm not losing my mind, I don't want to lose my mind Kjell Bjarne, I can't not again. I'll go mad.

Enter FRANK ÅSLI

KJELL: Frank. It's Christmas.

FRANK slams down letter on table

FRANK: Four thousand kroner. Four thousand kroner phone bill. Pussy talk or an apartment. The choice was yours. You don't meet people over the phone. It's a matter of prioritising.

ELLING: That's what I'm always telling Kjell Bjarne. Prioritise, prioritise, prioritise.

KJELL: I've never heard that.

ELLING: Yes you have.

FRANK: Enough. You had your chance. On with your coats, I'm taking you back.

KJELL: But, Frank.

FRANK: Coat, now Kjell Bjarne.

KJELL: Yes, Frank Åsli.

KJELL goes upstage

Gets coat out of wardrobe

Puts it on

FRANK lights up cigarette

ELLING: You win, Frank.

FRANK: No. This way nobody wins.

ELLING: Maybe I just don't belong in the real world, Frank.

ELLING takes coat off back of chair

FRANK: Give me one good reason why I should let you stay.

KJELL BJARNE returns downstage

KJELL: I'm ready.

FRANK: Well, one good reason.

Silence

ELLING: Kjell Bjarne has a girlfriend.

KJELL: No, I don't.

ELLING: Yes, he does. Her name's Reidun. She lives upstairs.

FRANK: Is this true, Kjell Bjarne.

KJELL: We just met.

ELLING: She's invited him to dinner.

FRANK: Great, that's great Kjell Bjarne.

KJELL: She's pregnant.

FRANK: Congratulations. Quick work. Elling.

Silence

ELLING: Nothing, Frank. A cigar. Have a cigar.

Gives FRANK cigar

FRANK: Where did you get this from.

ELLING: I bought it.

FRANK: No, you didn't.

ELLING: Yes, I did Frank.

KJELL: He did, Frank.

FRANK: No, he didn't – not unless you've both been to Cuba without telling me, or know a specialist supplier. And they cost a small fortune.

Telephone rings

ELLING: I'll get it.

Picks up receiver

Hello… Yes… Yes – Elling speaking… Well, happy Christmas to you as well Alfons –

Puts hand over mouthpiece

It's my friend, Alfons, he's rung to say happy Christmas… Oh, a colleague of mine Alfons, and a business associate…

FRANK: Elling has made a friend.

KJELL: Yes, Frank, he has.

FRANK: He hasn't made him up.

KJELL: No, Frank, he has not.

ELLING: Give me your number (*To FRANK.*) Frank, Frank, pen, paper, quick – Alfons is giving me his number…

FRANK gives telephone bill and pen to ELLING

… Shoot…

ELLING writes

FRANK: It looks like you boys are doing better than I thought.

KJELL: Really, Frank.

FRANK: Really.

KJELL: Holy shit.

ELLING: Right away, Alfons.

Puts down phone

I am afraid I shall be unable to accompany you to the asylum Frank, as a friend of mine is having a spot of bother and requires my help.

FRANK: Keep the pen.

ELLING: Keep the cigar. Oh, and Kjell Bjarne, if you would kindly refrain from cursing when I'm on the phone to my friends I'd be most grateful.

Goes into bedroom and changes

FRANK: No more pussy talk.

Exit FRANK

Silence

KJELL makes to exit

KJELL: I'm going to the shop.

ELLING: Good, good.

KJELL: You've got a friend.

ELLING: Yes, Kjell Bjarne.

KJELL: You're going to see him.

ELLING: Yes, Kjell Bjarne.

KJELL: I'll come with you, if you like.

ELLING: No. You have Reidun's leaky plumbing to fix.

KJELL: I could skip the plumbing.

ELLING: No. You must. You have to. You want to.

KJELL: She likes me.

ELLING: What about the baby's father.

KJELL: That damn Spaniard. If that bastard shows up here, he's in deep shit. Imagine knocking her up like that.

ELLING: Yes, imagine.

KJELL: And then taking off. I'll see she's alright. I'll look after that baby like it was my own.

ELLING: So, now you're going to marry her. You've only just met. You know nothing about her.

KJELL: I know she works at a laundromat.

ELLING: How can you trust her.

KJELL: I like her.

ELLING: How do you know she isn't using you to get to me.

KJELL: She doesn't know you.

ELLING: Exactly, I'm an enigma.

KJELL: I like her, I like her a lot.

ELLING: Then tell her.

KJELL: I don't know how to.

ELLING: How stupid can you be.

KJELL: I'm no good at talking. I don't know what to say.

ELLING: That's probably why she likes you, the strong silent type – mysterious.

KJELL: That's good?

ELLING: Just go to the shop.

KJELL: I'll get some stewed prunes, I'm having trouble.

ELLING: I have no wish to know.

Exit KJELL

You're actually doing better, Elling, you know that. I am. You are. I know. Angst is the price you have to pay. All I have to do is find a forum for my poetry.

Doorbell

Silence

Maybe they'll go away.

Doorbell

Hello, who is it.

REIDUN: (*Off.*) Reidun Nordsletten, from the apartment above.

ELLING: Kjell Bjarne is out, he's gone to the shop.

REIDUN: I know. I saw him go.

69

ELLING: (*To self.*) God help me, I'm at the centre of a love triangle.

REIDUN: Are you Elling.

ELLING: Yes, I am Elling.

REIDUN: It's you I want. Let me in.

ELLING: (*To self.*) It's one thing to break all boundaries, but quite another to blow your life to smithereens.

REIDUN: I need to talk.

ELLING: Come in.

Enter REIDUN

REIDUN: I have to talk to you about Kjell Bjarne.

ELLING: And that is all.

REIDUN: Yes.

ELLING: Nothing else.

REIDUN: No.

ELLING: Oh.

REIDUN: You know him better than anyone. I need to ask you something.

ELLING: I can't just tell you anything about Kjell Bjarne.

REIDUN: Why not.

ELLING: Because a friendship between two men requires a level of confidentiality.

REIDUN: I just think he's so – so – very, very – odd.

ELLING: Odd.

REIDUN: Odd.

ELLING: I prefer the English expression 'rare'. Rare. As in uncommon.

REIDUN: That was beautifully put.

ELLING: Words are my forte.

REIDUN: He never says anything.

ELLING: Kjell Bjarne ruminates.

REIDUN: Ruminates.

ELLING: Ruminates. He tends to sit on things, and has a long fuse.

REIDUN: Has he had many women.

ELLING: That's not for me to say.

REIDUN: Do you think he likes me.

ELLING: No, Reidun Nordsletten. Kjell Bjarne loves you.

REIDUN: What did you say.

ELLING: I don't believe I just said that.

REIDUN: Has he said that he loves me.

ELLING: No. But I know Kjell Bjarne.

REIDUN: We've only just met.

ELLING: You don't reciprocate.

REIDUN: No, I do, I do – as soon as I first set eyes upon him I knew, I knew. He was heaven-sent.

ELLING: You must leave now. Kjell Bjarne may be back any second.

REIDUN: He can get that jealous.

ELLING: It's best not to challenge him.

REIDUN: Thank you.

She kisses him on the cheek

Thank you.

Enter KJELL with shopping

Oh, Kjell Bjarne. I was just going.

Exit REIDUN

ELLING: Kjell Bjarne, what sort of prunes did you get.

KJELL drops shopping

Grabs ELLING by the throat and pins him to the kitchen table and throttles him

71

Nothing happened – Kjell Bjarne – Kjell Bjarne – you're killing me –

KJELL: Good.

ELLING: We just talked – I'm dying –

KJELL: Not yet, first you suffer –

ELLING: You're mad.

KJELL: Yes. I'll get off on grounds of 'diminished responsibility'.

ELLING: She wanted to talk about you – we talked about you – she loves you –

KJELL: I'll kill you.

ELLING: She loves you –

KJELL lets go

ELLING stands, recovers breath

She loves you Kjell Bjarne.

KJELL: She said that.

Telephone rings

ELLING answers

ELLING: Hello…yes…yes… Fine, fine thank you – I just ran up the stairs. How about you… It still hurts – remain seated… Of course – I'm on my way.

Puts phone down

Alfons. I have to go.

KJELL: Elling –

ELLING: He wants me to pick a few things up along the way.

KJELL: I didn't mean…

ELLING: I know.

KJELL: Is it true.

ELLING: I have to go out.

KJELL: I'll come with you.

ELLING: No. You wait here, Kjell Bjarne.

ELLING puts coat on and goes to exit

KJELL: Elling –

ELLING stops and turns

ELLING: Yes, Kjell Bjarne.

KJELL: Is it true that Reidun…

ELLING: It's true. She loves you. And I told her that you love her too.

Exit ELLING

KJELL: Holy shit.

KJELL sits at table

KJELL turns on radio

Music: 'You Don't Have to Say You Love Me', Dusty Springfield

Sits and listens

(At end of first verse.) Holy shit.

And turns radio up – just before first line of chorus

Volume increases steadily

(Just before second chorus.) Elling.

Exit KJELL BJARNE

ALFONS sits on downstage right chair facing out front

Right leg up on a pile of books

Enter ELLING with carrier bag

Music out

ALFONS: Here I sit, like another idiot.

ELLING: Have you broken something.

ALFONS: I hope not. I sprained it while chasing the kids off my car in the courtyard down below. Damn kids. They're another species.

ELLING: All these books.

ALFONS: Poetry. It's an obsession.

ELLING: Do you know any.

ALFONS: Poets. Some.

ELLING: And have you ever, yourself.

ALFONS: Committed an act of poetry.

ELLING: Yes.

ALFONS: It has been known. I have dabbled. And you.

ELLING: I keep a notebook.

ALFONS: Oh, yes. Did you remember the beer.

ELLING: Yes.

Gives ALFONS a can

Both open their cans

ALFONS: You don't drink.

ELLING: I need a drink.

ALFONS: Oh, like that is it.

ELLING: Something.

ALFONS: Cheers.

ELLING: Cheers.

They drink

You can't walk on this foot.

ALFONS: No. But I have a friend to help me. A friend with literary ambitions.

ELLING: Will you introduce us.

ALFONS: As a younger man I dabbled – I carried a notebook everywhere I went and was always writing things down. A cornucopia of momentary visions, random thoughts, observations, intoxicating feelings. I wrote everything down

ELLING: Yes, yes.

ALFONS: My notebook became my friend and I felt bereft without it.

ELLING: You understand.

ALFONS: I understand.

ELLING: And now.

ALFONS: One day I stopped. It stopped. Now I take life as it comes.

ELLING: So many books.

ALFONS: Books don't let you down. You can depend on a book. Books don't go away. Guard that notebook with your life. Show it no one, people will ask – at all costs resist the urge.

ELLING: Sometimes, I do get the urge.

ALFONS: Resist. They wouldn't understand.

ELLING: But you would.

ALFONS: Yes, I would have a certain understanding. But I wouldn't dream of asking.

ELLING: But if I wanted to.

ALFONS: I would be honoured. You could leave it with me, so that I could study it over a few days.

ELLING: Maybe –

ELLING reaches inside jacket for notebook

Clattering of bins outside

ALFONS: Damn kids.

ELLING: They're still there.

More clattering

ALFONS: Lean out the window and tell them to clear off.

ELLING looks out front

ELLING: You down, there – yes you, come out – have you no respect for the elderly – Kjell Bjarne, is that you – what are you doing down there.

ALFONS: Who is it. You know him.

ELLING: Kjell Bjarne, I share an apartment with him.

ALFONS: Tell him to come up.

Enter KJELL BJARNE

ELLING turns upstage

ELLING: Alfons Jorgensen, Kjell Bjarne. Kjell Bjarne, Alfons Jorgensen.

KJELL: Hi.

ELLING: Are you spying on me.

KJELL: No, I was looking at that old car in the courtyard down below.

ELLING: I can take care of myself. I'm visiting a friend.

KJELL: A drinking buddy.

ELLING: Yes.

ALFONS: I needed Elling to get me some shopping. Give Kjell Bjarne a beer.

ELLING: The bag's over there.

KJELL takes a beer

KJELL: Thank you, Alfons.

Opens beer

You've hurt your foot.

ALFONS: Chasing kids off my car, in the courtyard below.

KJELL: She belongs to you. What a beauty.

ELLING: It's just an old car.

KJELL: Fifty-nine Buick Century Hardtop.

ALFONS: Fifty-eight. We bought it in sixty-two.

ELLING: Alfons is not interested in cars, are you Alfons. Alfons is interested in poetry.

ALFONS: I'm interested in both. It's rusty and old, I haven't driven it since my wife died.

KJELL: I can bring her back to life.

ALFONS: My wife, or the Buick.

KJELL: The Buick.

ALFONS: You can try. I fear it's too late.

KJELL: Holy shit.

ALFONS: Eva died in seventy-nine, and so did the car.

ELLING: Mother died exactly two years and six months ago today.

Silence

ALFONS: It happens.

Silence

KJELL: I know I can bring her back to life.

ALFONS: Feel free to work on it any time you like.

ELLING: He'll never get it to start.

KJELL: Sure I will.

ALFONS: Sure he will. And when he has, I'm inviting you for a drive. Something for you to write about in your notebook.

ELLING: A drive. Do you mean…?

KJELL: He means a drive. Where you drive around in a car until you're done.

ALFONS: We can go to my cabin. I haven't been there for years.

ELLING: We've been invited to his cabin, Kjell Bjarne.

KJELL: A cabin. If Frank will allow us.

ELLING: This is none of Frank's business.

ALFONS: Who is Frank

ELLING: It's time we cut Frank Åsli down to size. I won't let the welfare state stop me. Why can't I go to someone's cabin. I have never been to a cabin in my life. Never. Does that welfare rat get to decide what I can and cannot do.

ALFONS: I see.

77

ELLING: Do you Alfons.

ALFONS: Yes. When the time is right, you talk to Frank – tell him to call me. But first we fix the car. One step at a time.

KJELL: Where did you get all these books.

ALFONS: They just came flying.

ELLING: A lot of poetry.

ALFONS: Take what you want. Now, if you don't mind I need to lie down.

KJELL: Where's the bedroom.

ALFONS: Down there.

KJELL: I'll give you a hand.

ALFONS: Remember, guard that notebook with your life and show it no one.

Exit KJELL with ALFONS

ELLING picks up a book from pile ALFONS had his foot on

ELLING: (*Reads cover.*) 'They Fuck You Up'.

Enter KJELL

KJELL: I'll make her run if it's the last thing I do.

ELLING: You can do it, Kjell Bjarne.

KJELL: Sure I can.

ELLING: We have been invited to a cabin.

KJELL: I love that car. It's gorgeous.

ELLING: More so than Reidun Nordsletten.

KJELL: What are all these damn books for.

ELLING: Reading. And it's all poetry. You should focus on Reidun, not that car.

KJELL: I know I can make it work.

ELLING: And then we will go to a cabin. Imagine. You and me going to a cabin. That's the life Kjell Bjarne: cars, cabins, the open road, adventure. Let's go home.

KJELL: What about Alfons.

ELLING: Leave him to sleep. Let's go. Elling and Kjell Bjarne.

The city of Oslo's new emergency rescue team.

Pregnant or elderly, call day or night. A cabin, Kjell Bjarne.

KJELL: A cabin.

Act Four

ELLING in kitchen

Production line

Sauerkraut packets

Inserting poems

KJELL BJARNE upstage

In bed groaning

ELLING: My entire life I have respected the efforts of the labour movement.

KJELL groans

Idleness has always been my worst enemy.

KJELL groans

I need projects. And this is my greatest. I have found the forum for my poetry – sauerkraut. Purchase, open, insert and reseal. Each packet of sauerkraut primed with a poem. Surreptitiously placed on the shelves of randomly selected supermarkets, thereby avoiding the discovery of any discernable pattern by the authorities.

KJELL groans

KJELL: I'm dying.

ELLING: You're not dying. Sauerkraut, my forum.

KJELL: I'm dying.

ELLING: Winter is nearly gone, soon spring will be here, new life bursting out all over the place, get up, go out, celebrate.

KJELL groans

KJELL: I prefer it when you're miserable.

ELLING: I'm never miserable. Misery is a product of self-pity. I feel gloomy, I get up, I get on, I don't lie in bed feeling sorry for myself.

KJELL: No, you climb in the wardrobe and shut the door behind you.

ELLING: There is no wardrobe big enough in the whole of Norway that could contain me now.

KJELL groans

KJELL: I'm dying.

ELLING: If you keep that groaning up, you will get dizzy and...vomit.

KJELL: I can't take it anymore.

ELLING: You aren't getting any more clear-headed.

KJELL: Help me, Elling.

ELLING: Do something to impress her.

KJELL: I don't know what to say.

ELLING: Let go, Kjell Bjarne. Improvise.

KJELL: Improvise.

ELLING: Improvise. Feast on love.

KJELL: This isn't food. If only she was.

Doorbell goes

ELLING goes to answer it

ELLING: Don't be absurd, Kjell Bjarne – would you really prefer that Reidun was a sausage.

KJELL: Don't. I'm hungry and I can't eat.

Enter FRANK with ELLING

FRANK: I came as soon as I could. What's the matter.

ELLING: I can't get him to get up, he's been lying in bed groaning for four days now.

KJELL groans

FRANK: He's in your bedroom.

ELLING: We prefer it that way.

FRANK goes into bedroom

FRANK: Are you sick, Kjell Bjarne.

KJELL: No. I'm dying.

ELLING: He won't even get up for a game of Parcheesi.

FRANK: Are you feeling unwell.

KJELL: No.

KJELL groans

FRANK: What's the matter.

ELLING: Kjell Bjarne is in love.

KJELL: No, I'm not.

ELLING: You are.

FRANK: The woman that invited you to dinner.

ELLING: Reidun.

KJELL groans

FRANK: You went. He went.

ELLING: Yes, he went. That was two months ago.

FRANK: What happened.

KJELL: She gave me some sort of steamed jam pudding with custard. The best damn pudding I ever had.

KJELL groans

I'm hungry.

ELLING: Then eat.

KJELL: I can't.

ELLING: Then starve.

KJELL: I'm dying.

FRANK: And since dinner.

ELLING: Nothing. She's about to have a baby.

FRANK: It's obvious what is wrong with Kjell Bjarne.

ELLING: He's stupid and is unable to hold a conversation with her.

FRANK: No, he feels displaced by the imminent arrival of Reidun's baby, and therefore is behaving like a baby

himself in order to compete for Reidun's attention.
Starving himself till she feeds him.

ELLING: With what.

FRANK: The 'good breast'.

ELLING: No wonder the country's in a state. No, Frank, he just doesn't know what say to her.

KJELL: What was that about a 'good breast'.

ELLING: He says you're jealous of the baby.

KJELL: That damn Spaniard, he comes anywhere near the baby and I'll knock his block off.

ELLING: See, Frank.

FRANK: How about group therapy.

ELLING: No, Frank, what he needs to do is to speak to her. You have to invite her to dinner, to a movie, or something. Now, Kjell Bjarne.

KJELL: Do I have to.

ELLING: Yes, now.

ELLING pulls back KJELL's sheets

KJELL: Can't you go instead.

ELLING: Get out of bed.

KJELL: I need a bath.

ELLING: You don't wash.

KJELL: I've decided to start.

ELLING: Go and ask her out.

KJELL: What do I say.

ELLING: Just ask her out.

FRANK: Now, Kjell Bjarne.

KJELL: Yes, Frank Åsli.

Exit KJELL

FRANK: Do you have anything on the go.

ELLING: Yes, Frank.

FRANK: That's nice. How's your friend, Alfons.

ELLING: Yes, fine. Kjell Bjarne is fixing up his car for him.

FRANK: Kjell Bjarne is a mechanic.

ELLING: Yes, Frank.

FRANK: Who is Alfons.

ELLING: Alfons Jorgensen.

FRANK: Alfons Jorgensen.

ELLING: What's wrong with him.

FRANK: Nothing.

ELLING: You know him.

FRANK: He's quite a famous poet. But he hasn't written anything for years. His wife died and he stopped writing. There was no logic to it.

ELLING: Logic is the enemy of reason, Frank.

FRANK: I'm not your enemy, Elling.

ELLING: No, Frank.

FRANK: What's all the sauerkraut for.

ELLING: I'm laying down supplies for next winter.

FRANK: Watch it, I've got my eye on you – behave.

ELLING: I always do.

FRANK begins to exit

Enter KJELL as he does

KJELL: I did it.

FRANK: You never told me you were a mechanic, Kjell Bjarne.

KJELL: You never asked.

FRANK: You should have told me.

KJELL: Yes, Frank Åsli

Exit FRANK

ELLING: I don't trust that man.

KJELL: I did it, Elling. I did it, and it was done.

ELLING: What, what, did what – now what have you done.

KJELL: Invited her out

Knocking at door

Enter REIDUN

REIDUN: Kjell Bjarne.

KJELL: Reidun.

REIDUN: Elling.

ELLING: Good afternoon, Reidun.

REIDUN: Thanks for the invitation.

ELLING: Don't thank me. Thank Kjell Bjarne.

KJELL: No, thank Elling.

REIDUN: Yes. But what time, Kjell Bjarne.

KJELL: Reidun wants to know when.

ELLING: You didn't say when.

KJELL: No, I asked her out.

ELLING: Well, how about now.

KJELL: Now.

ELLING: Yes, now.

KJELL: How about now.

REIDUN: Yes, Kjell Bjarne, now will be fine. Can I get my coat.

KJELL BJARNE looks at ELLING

ELLING: Yes.

KJELL: Yes.

REIDUN: Thank you. Thank you, Elling.

ELLING: Have fun.

REIDUN: I will.

Exit REIDUN

KJELL: Wait. Reidun. Wait for me. Elling. Come with us.

ELLING: I can't, I have work to do.

Exit KJELL

ELLING goes over to table and picks up packet of sauerkraut

No one knows it yet, but the city has a new poet: The Sauerkraut Poet. The enigmatic 'E' is about to strike.

Puts on sunglasses

Music

Puts on coat

Sets to work removing sauerkraut packets

Lights dim from day through to early evening

ELLING at kitchen table

One packet of sauerkraut left

Takes off sunglasses

Picks up sauerkraut

The last drop.

Enter REIDUN chased by KJELL

REIDUN: No – Kjell Bjarne –

KJELL: Now I've got you.

REIDUN: Don't – don't –

He chases her round room

No – no –

ELLING enters from kitchen

Holding packet of sauerkraut

ELLING: So, you're back.

KJELL: Elling.

ELLING: Back from going out.

KJELL: Yes.

ELLING: Have a good time.

KJELL: The best. I showed Reidun the Buick.

REIDUN: What a great car. It's so big inside, like a ballroom.

ELLING: Americans are generous people. You went to see Alfons.

KJELL: Yes.

REIDUN: He's such a cutie.

ELLING: Did you have an invite.

KJELL: No we just dropped by. I was working on the car.

REIDUN: So we rang on his bell. He didn't mind.

ELLING: Alfons is polite.

REIDUN: No, he really was pleased to see Kjell Bjarne.

KJELL: He said Reidun could drop by any time she likes.

REIDUN: He's such a cutie.

ELLING: So you keep saying. You shouldn't pester Alfons.

KJELL: Reidun washed his whole apartment.

ELLING: I have to go.

Slips sauerkraut inside his coat

And puts on sunglasses

REIDUN: What are you doing.

ELLING: Nothing, it's private.

REIDUN: You're wearing sunglasses.

ELLING: I have been out. Delivering packages. And am about to do so again. I have one more delivery to make, and must get there before the shop shuts.

KJELL: His foot is a lot better.

ELLING: He showed you his foot.

REIDUN: I'll go upstairs.

ELLING: Yes, you go upstairs and Kjell Bjarne will follow you no doubt as he is your friend. As in a like way, but not altogether similar – for neither of us are pregnant and we are both men – Alfons and I are friends.

REIDUN: Goodnight, Kjell Bjarne.

KJELL: Goodnight, Reidun.

ELLING: See, you can even communicate with her of your own accord, you don't need me.

REIDUN: Goodnight, Elling.

ELLING: Goodbye, Reidun.

Exit REIDUN

I see your game –

KJELL: Calm, calm.

ELLING: Don't tell me to calm.

KJELL: Calm down, Elling.

ELLING: I am calm. I'm calm. Alright.

KJELL: Alright.

ELLING: Give me a cigarette.

KJELL: You don't smoke.

ELLING: You're trying to take over my friend Alfons Jorgensen. Pretending he's your friend, that it's your car…

KJELL: I wasn't pretending anything. It's you that makes things up.

ELLING: I'm a poet. He feels pressured, you're putting too much pressure on him. Behaving like you've known each other for ever. At least I have my poetry to myself, no one can take that away from me

KJELL: Alfons has invited us all to his cabin this weekend.

ELLING: This weekend.

KJELL: This weekend.

ELLING: You've fixed the car.

KJELL: I fixed the car.

ELLING: Kjell Bjarne you are a genius.

KJELL: Holy shit.

ELLING: We're going away.

KJELL: Yes.

ELLING: To a cabin.

KJELL: Yes. In a car.

ELLING: In the country. In a cabin.

KJELL: Yes. You, me, Reidun, and the baby.

ELLING: Why does she have to come.

KJELL: Reidun's my friend.

ELLING: I'm not taking a friend.

KJELL: Alfons is your friend.

ELLING: Yes, he is. A weekend in the country. If Frank will allow it.

Blackout

Telephone rings

The following as voice-over

Hello, Elling speaking.

FRANK: Hi, it's me, Frank. Now about this weekend –

ELLING: Listen, Frank –

FRANK: You guys had better behave –

ELLING: You can't stop us.

FRANK: Behave yourselves on your cabin trip.

Music – 'Driving Along in My Automobile'

Lights up

KJELL and REIDUN push his bed downstage right

ELLING's remains upstage left

Table centre

Enter ELLING with sleeping bag

ELLING: Tonight I'm going to walk along the shore like a sober Dylan Thomas.

KJELL and ALFONS move table and chairs centre stage

REIDUN: This is beautiful.

ALFONS: It should be alright, as long as the previous tenants didn't burn everything to keep themselves warm.

ELLING: Is it because I finally am getting out that everything conspired to stop me from getting here, even the police.

ALFONS: They were after me, the driver, not you.

KJELL: It's good that nobody had been drinking.

ELLING: So I'm not interesting, just because I sit on the back seat. I have had more than my fair share of encounters with the criminal 'injustice' system. Not enough to make me an outlaw as such, I will admit – but enough to make me known. Interpol will be aware of me. Shortly after mother's death the police abducted me from my apartment. I am probably under surveillance.

REIDUN: It was a routine check, license and registration.

ELLING: To the undiscerning eye, maybe. But did you not think it was odd the way he knew so much about the particulars of your car Alfons.

ALFONS: He was just an enthusiast.

ELLING: And a policeman. Policemen are never 'just', they are always something. My suspicions were aroused by his opening gambit, 'Nice set of wheels'.

ALFONS: He was just being friendly.

ELLING: Notice how he did nothing to stop me when I raised the bonnet and asked him to check out the tefting.

REIDUN: That's because you were talking twaddle.

ELLING: It was then that he let us on our way.

REIDUN: He felt sorry for us.

ELLING: I had blown his cover.

KJELL: It was the radiator pipe.

ELLING: Where I come from we call it 'tefting'.

ALFONS: Do you know how to sail, Elling.

KJELL: Elling's an old sailor. Ask him about the Caribbean, Alf.

ELLING downstage right with sleeping bag

REIDUN upstage left with bedding

KJELL centre stage

Where am I sleeping, Alf.

ALFONS: Wherever. I have three bedrooms.

ELLING: We can stay in here, Kjell Bjarne.

REIDUN: Here's our room, Kjell Bjarne.

ELLING: You realise that's not possible.

KJELL: This is none of your business.

ELLING: She's sick, you're sick – it's sick. How dare you even consider it. You'll crush the baby.

REIDUN: You won't need a sleeping bag.

ELLING: You're willing to become a murderer for some kinky sex.

REIDUN: I'll make our bed.

REIDUN goes to upstage left bed and strips it

ELLING: Don't do it.

ALFONS: I'm just popping into town to get some more wine.

Exit ALFONS

KJELL joins REIDUN upstage left

ELLING: Murderer.

Music

REIDUN and KJELL make bed

ELLING lays out sleeping bag downstage front

Sits on it, takes out notebook and pen

ELLING: (*Reads.*) 'Some days are beautiful
Other days it is not

To have coped with what we have
had to cope with
To have borne the burden with which
we are born
And in between…something…something
…and tea
Mother, I have not forgot'

KJELL and REIDUN set table

When set, they sit at table. REIDUN lights cigarette

Enter ALFONS with newspaper

Upstage in darkness

ALFONS: Elling.

ELLING puts notebook under sleeping bag

It's peaceful down here by the lake.

ELLING: Yes. I thought I might sleep out.

ALFONS: A good place to write. Under the moonlight.

ELLING: Yes.

ALFONS: Dinner. Oh, yes – I thought you might like a look at this.

I got it in town.

Gives paper to ELLING

There. 'The Sauerkraut Poet'.

ELLING: (*Reads.*) 'Kare Svingen, age twenty-seven, got more than she bargained for when she opened her usual packet of sauerkraut – '

ALFONS: A poem. And they've printed it. All of it, signed 'E'.

ELLING: (*Reads.*) 'All over Norway thousands are asking who is the mysterious underground poet "E". He is on everyone's lips. He has made his debut. When will he strike next.'

ALFONS: It must be tempting for him to step forward.

ELLING: No, he must remain anonymous, remain who he is.

ALFONS: Dinner.

ELLING and ALFONS join KJELL and REIDUN at table

KJELL: That's what Frank Åsli said.

ALFONS: 'Quite famous'.

KJELL: Those were his exact words to Elling, 'Alfons is quite famous' –

ALFONS: I see.

KJELL: Weren't they, Elling.

ELLING: Something like that.

KJELL: And that you stopped.

ALFONS: I didn't stop. It stopped. My wife died and everything stopped. My muse had deserted me.

ELLING: I'll clear the table.

ALFONS: Why so soon, Elling, relax. Sit down. Have a drink.

ALFONS fills ELLING's glass

ELLING sits

ELLING: I know my responsibilities. Reidun cooks, I clean up the mess.

KJELL: The best damn stew I ever had. Where did you learn to cook like that.

REIDUN: Domestic science.

ALFONS: I didn't learn anything at school.

REIDUN: School was rubbish.

ELLING: You learnt to cook. Both Reidun and Kjell Bjarne are good with their hands, Alfons.

REIDUN: It's a knack.

ELLING: They practise on her sofa.

KJELL: The government sent me to a special school, where they only taught idiots.

ALFONS: My parents sent me to a special school, where only idiots taught.

ELLING: Kjell Bjarne learned to read when he got his first dirty magazine.

REIDUN: The Labour Party is to blame for our lousy schooling.

ELLING: No, I won't let you say that, I won't let you get away with that – both mother, and I – don't blame the Labour Party for this.

REIDUN: They were in power.

ELLING: A house isn't in poor condition because of a few rotten boards.

ALFONS: He's speaking in pictures.

ELLING: And where did the rotten boards come from.

REIDUN: The lumber yard.

ALFONS: Very good, I like it. Have some more wine.

KJELL: Not for Elling.

ELLING: I am my own person, a free agent, fill her up.

ALFONS: You're sure.

KJELL: Elling.

ELLING: I'm sure.

ALFONS: Why not, it's good to let your hair down.

REIDUN: Depends how much you've got.

ELLING: I am not going bald.

REIDUN: I never said you were.

KJELL: No, she didn't.

ELLING: What do you know, murderer.

ALFONS: Oh, good, we're in for a stormy night.

ELLING: And who smuggled the rotten boards onto the construction site.

KJELL: Leave it, Elling.

ELLING: No. She's so clever. You're so clever Reidun, with your domestic science – you say, say where these rotten planks come from.

REIDUN: The lumber yard. Social democratic labourers from the Labour Party.

ELLING: No! They were bought and paid for by the CIA and the KGB. They brought the rotten boards.

REIDUN: So, why shout at me. Call them and shout.

Exit REIDUN to upstage left bed

KJELL: You shouldn't have done that.

KJELL stands

ELLING: Kjell Bjarne –

KJELL: I'm going to bed.

ELLING: You weigh two hundred pounds.

KJELL goes upstage left

Murderer.

ALFONS: Let's get drunk. You and me. Chew the fat. Against the world and modern poetry. Who knows, you might even show me some of what you've got written in that notebook of yours. Let's get plastered.

ELLING: No, thank you Alfons. I'm going out. I'll go out. To walk along the shore. The rocky shore.

ELLING walks downstage to sleeping bag

ALFONS fades into darkness (upstage not lit)

It had to happen. It had to come.The moment when Kjell Bjarne had to choose. He chose.

At first we crawl…then we stumble…and fall – But when night comes…at the end – as in the begining…

Enter KJELL

KJELL: Elling.

ELLING: Kjell Bjarne. My dear fellow –

KJELL: I have to get back.

ELLING: Oh.

Silence

What.

KJELL: Nothing.

ELLING: What do you want.

KJELL: Nothing.

ELLING: Then, go to bed.

KJELL: Can I borrow your underpants.

ELLING: Certainly not.

KJELL: But mine are dirty.

ELLING: You should have thought of that.

KJELL: How was I to know, I couldn't possibly have known.

ELLING: How long have you had them on for.

KJELL: It's hard to say.

ELLING: Hard to keep track of the weeks…

KJELL: I thought I'd be sharing with you.

ELLING: Oh, I see. And I don't count…

KJELL: No. Yes.

ELLING: How about my socks as well.

KJELL: Sure.

ELLING starts to take off trousers

ELLING: Well, don't just stand there, take off your pants.

KJELL: Sure.

Both take off underpants and exchange

KJELL puts on ELLING's

Feel free to use mine in whatever way you see fit.

ELLING: I'll put them on my head…

KJELL: If you like. There, how do I look.

ELLING: 'Rare', as the English say. As in uncommon.

KJELL: Thanks.

ELLING: No. Thank me properly, Kjell Bjarne.

KJELL offers his hand

KJELL: Thank you.

Silence

They shake

Exit KJELL upstage left into darkness

ELLING: Thank you, Kjell Bjarne. And good luck.

ELLING lies down on sleeping bag

And tries to sleep

Music

As lights dim from upstage darkness the following is heard

KJELL: No – no – Goddam – holy – holy – yes – yes – yes –
Holy shit – Yes – Ellllllllling!

Silence

Front stage light changes night to dawn

ALFONS: (*Off.*) Elling.

KJELL: (*Off.*) Elling.

ALFONS: (*Off.*) Elling.

KJELL: (*Off.*) Elling.

Enter KJELL

There you are.

ELLING: So, my underwear worked wonders.

KJELL: It's started.

ELLING: Screaming my name like that.

KJELL: You heard.

ELLING: Along with the rest of Norway.

KJELL: It's started. Reidun has started.

ELLING: Reidun's having her baby as we speak.

KJELL: We called an ambulance. They've taken her back to
Oslo. There's a complication. It's my fault – you said, and
you were right.

ELLING: Nonsense Kjell Bjarne. It's because of her age. There's always more chance of a complication.

ALFONS: (*Off.*) Elling. Kjell Bjarne.

KJELL: Alfons is waiting out front in the car.

ELLING: Then we had better hurry.

KJELL: What about your underpants.

ELLING: Keep them.

Exit ELLING and KJELL

Enter ALFONS

ALFONS: (*Shouts.*) Elling.

Picks up ELLING's sleeping bag

Sees notebook on ground

Picks it up

Elling. My muse.

Exit ALFONS

Music

Lights up

ELLING and KJELL sitting at table centre stage

Empty bottles of wine and telephone

Drinking from very large glasses

KJELL: She could give birth any second – thirty-six hours five minutes and…and…the damn thing keeps moving… seconds. What does hydrocephalic mean –

ELLING: Have another drink.

KJELL: Do something.

ELLING: I am.

Fills their glasses

KJELL knocks it back in one

KJELL: Where is Alfons.

ELLING: He went home.

Enter ALFONS downstage right

Puts ELLING's notebook on floor in front of chair

Sits and looks at notebook

Takes out hip flask

And drinks

Looks at notebook

ALFONS: 'Inside The Mind Of A Madman', a new collection of poems by Alfons Jorgensen.

KJELL: I'm going to be a father.

ELLING: You're drunk.

KJELL: I'm not drunk.

ELLING: You get drunk, and you'll get sent right back to the asylum.

Have another drink. I'll have another drink.

Fills their glasses

ALFONS: 'The Diary of A Madman', by Alfons Jorgensen.

ELLING: Cheers.

KJELL: Cheers.

They drink

ALFONS: 'The Work of A Madman', by Alfons Jorgensen.

Goes to pick up notebook

No.

Sits and looks at notebook

Phone rings. KJELL answers it

No. Damn you Elling. Damn you. Damn, damn, damn.

Puts on coat

Picks up notebook

Damn fool.

Exit ALFONS

Silence

KJELL replaces receiver

Silence

ELLING: Well.

Silence

KJELL: It's a girl. Over ten pounds, Elling. A huge girl. Did you hear that, Elling. Over ten pounds.

ELLING: She's going to be bigger than you, Kjell Bjarne.

KJELL: Elling – Elling – Elling, you are a true friend whatever happens tomorrow, whatever they do to us, I want you to know that. I was cranky because I was scared. And then I met you. Mommy's boy.

ELLING: Now, sleep.

ELLING helps KJELL to his bed.

KJELL: Where are you sleeping.

ELLING: In my bedroom.

KJELL: In your bedroom.

ELLING: Yes.

KJELL: Close the door behind you.

ELLING: I will.

KJELL: Night, then.

ELLING: Night.

ELLING sits at table

Mommy's boy – 'E', the anonymous voice from the quiet streets of the night. But how much longer. For how much longer.

Falls asleep

Music

Night through to morning

Doorbell

ELLING wakes

Lights a cigarette

Doorbell

It's open.

Enter FRANK ÅSLI

Cigarette, Frank.

FRANK: I've given up. You don't smoke.

ELLING: No, I don't.

FRANK: There's vomit in the hall.

ELLING: Kjell Bjarne.

FRANK: This place is a tip.

ELLING: It was the alcohol.

FRANK: Where's Kjell Bjarne.

ELLING: In his bed.

FRANK: In his bedroom.

ELLING: Take us, Frank. We're ready.

FRANK: You really did it this time. You didn't give a damn.

ELLING: I'll wake Kjell Bjarne.

FRANK: Leave him. Clear up this vomit. And then you can read this.

Puts book on table

ELLING: Yes, Frank.

FRANK: But mind you take it back by the return date, it's a library book.

FRANK checks on KJELL

ELLING opens book

ELLING: 'Collected Works', Alfons Jorgensen.

FRANK: You sure he's not dead.

ELLING: Frank, Frank, the return date for this is three weeks.

FRANK: That's what I said, it's a library book.

ELLING: Well, I have to be here to take it back.

FRANK: Yeah.

ELLING: You're not taking us away.

FRANK: Where.

ELLING: The asylum.

FRANK: Asylums are for lunatics. Normal people push the boat out, celebrate, get drunk, drink too much and vomit when children are born. Take an aspirin, clean up. Congratulations. I'll be back.

Exit FRANK

ELLING goes and tries to wake KJELL

ELLING: Kjell Bjarne… Kjell Bjarne…wake up Kjell Bjarne – it's normal…we're normal –

Enter ALFONS

ALFONS: Hello.

ELLING: It's normal to vomit when you have children.

ALFONS: Hello.

ELLING leaves KJELL

ELLING: Alfons –

ALFONS: I know. I just met Frank Åsli. I think I taught him in the eighties. He hasn't changed. Good-natured scruff. The door was open. I found this.

Puts notebook on table

ELLING: You read it.

ALFONS: Tempted.

ALFONS turns and makes to go

Stops. Turns

Oh, the Sauerkraut Poet –

ELLING: Yes.

ALFONS: I forgot to say.

ELLING: What.

ALFONS: He's really rather good.

ELLING: You think.

ALFONS: I do.

Exit ALFONS

ELLING: Holy shit.

KJELL sits up

KJELL: Elling – I'm dying.

The end

Printed in the USA
CPSIA information can be obtained
at www.ICGtesting.com
LVHW020856171024
794056LV00002B/562

9 781840 027945